G000129398

♓ LOVE SIGNS ♓

PISCES

February 19 – March 20

JULIA & DEREK PARKER

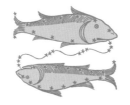

DK

Dedicated to Martin Lethbridge

A DK PUBLISHING BOOK

Project Editor • Annabel Morgan
Art Editor • Anna Benjamin
Managing Editor • Francis Ritter
Managing Art Editor • Derek Coombes
DTP Designer • Cressida Joyce
Production Controller • Martin Croshaw
US Editor • Constance M. Robinson

ACKNOWLEDGMENTS

Photography: Steve Gorton: pp. 10, 13–15, 17–19, 46–49; Ian O'Leary: 16. *Additional photography by:* Colin Keates, David King, Monique Le Luhandre, David Murray, Tim Ridley, Clive Streeter, Harry Taylor, Matthew Ward. *Artworks:* Nic Demin: 34–45; Peter Lawman: *jacket*, 4, 12; Paul Redgrave: 24–33; Satwinder Sehmi: *glyphs*; Jane Thomson: *borders*; Rosemary Woods: 11.

Peter Lawman's paintings are exhibited by the Portal Gallery Ltd, London.

Picture credits: Bridgeman Art Library/Hermitage, St. Petersburg: 51; Robert Harding Picture Library: 20l, 20c, 20r; Images Colour Library: 9; The National Gallery, London: 11; The Royal Geographical Society: 48br; Tony Stone Images: 21t, 21b; The Victoria and Albert Museum, London: 5; Zefa: 21c.

ISBN 0-7894-1088-5

Reproduced by Bright Arts, Hong Kong
Printed and bound by Imago, Hong Kong

CONTENTS

Astrology & You 8

Looking for a Lover 10

You & Your Lover 12

The Food of Love 16

Places to Love 20

Venus & Mars 22

Your Love Life 24

Your Sex Life 34

Tokens of Love 46

Your Permanent Relationship 50

Venus & Mars Tables 52

ASTROLOGY & YOU

THERE IS MUCH MORE TO ASTROLOGY THAN YOUR SUN SIGN.
A SIMPLE INVESTIGATION INTO THE POSITION OF THE OTHER
PLANETS AT THE MOMENT OF YOUR BIRTH WILL PROVIDE YOU
WITH FASCINATING INSIGHTS INTO YOUR PERSONALITY.

*Y*our birth sign, or Sun sign, is the sign of the zodiac that the Sun occupied at the moment of your birth. The majority of books on astrology concentrate only on explaining the relevance of the Sun signs. This is a simple form of astrology that can provide you with some interesting but rather general information about you and your personality. In this book, we take you a step further, and reveal how the planets Venus and Mars work in association with your Sun sign to influence your attitudes toward romance and sexuality.

In order to gain a detailed insight into your personality, a "natal" horoscope, or birth chart, is necessary. This details the position of all the planets in our solar system at the moment of your birth, not just the position of the Sun. Just as the Sun occupied one of the 12 zodiac signs when you were born, perhaps making you "a Geminian" or "a Sagittarian," so each of the other planets occupied a certain sign. Each planet governs a different area of your personality, and the planets Venus and Mars are responsible for your attitudes toward love and sex, respectively.

For example, if you are a Sun-sign Sagittarian, according to the attributes of the sign you should be a dynamic, freedom-loving character. However, if Venus occupied Libra when you were born, you may make a passive and clinging partner – qualities that are supposedly completely alien to Sagittarians.

A MAP OF THE CONSTELLATION

*The 16th-century astronomer Copernicus first made the
revolutionary suggestion that the planets orbit the Sun
rather than Earth. In this 17th-century constellation chart,
the Sun is shown at the center of the solar system.*

The tables on pages 52–61 of this book will enable you to discover the positions of Mars and Venus at the moment of your birth. Once you have read this information, turn to pages 22–45. On these pages we explain how the influences of Venus and Mars interact with the characteristics of your Sun sign. This information will provide you with many illuminating insights into your personality, and explains how the planets have formed your attitudes toward love and sex.

LOOKING FOR A LOVER

ASTROLOGY CAN PROVIDE YOU WITH VALUABLE INFORMATION
ON HOW TO INITIATE AND MAINTAIN RELATIONSHIPS. IT CAN
ALSO TELL YOU HOW COMPATIBLE YOU ARE WITH YOUR LOVER,
AND HOW SUCCESSFUL YOUR RELATIONSHIP IS LIKELY TO BE.

*P*eople frequently use astrology to lead into a relationship, and "What sign are you?" is often used as a conversation opener. Some people simply introduce the subject as an opening gambit, while others place great importance on this question and its answer.

Astrology can affect the way you think and behave when you are in love. It can also provide you with fascinating information about your lovers and your relationships. Astrology cannot tell you who to fall in love with or who to avoid, but it can offer you some very helpful advice.

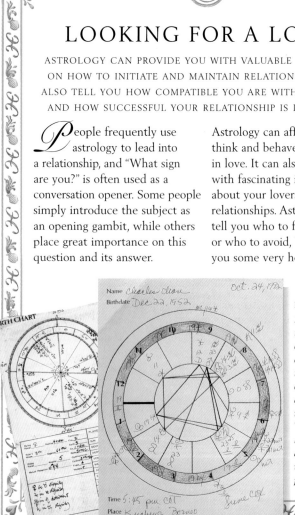

BIRTH CHARTS
*Synastry involves
the comparison
of two people's
charts in order
to assess their
compatibility in
all areas of their
relationship.
The process can
highlight any
areas of common
interest or
potential conflict.*

THE TABLE OF ELEMENTS

People whose signs are grouped under the same element tend to find it easy to fall into a happy relationship. The groupings are:

FIRE: *Aries, Leo, Sagittarius*
EARTH: *Taurus, Virgo, Capricorn*
AIR: *Gemini, Libra, Aquarius*
WATER: *Cancer, Scorpio, Pisces*

When you meet someone to whom you are attracted, astrology can provide you with a valuable insight into his or her personality. It may even reveal unattractive characteristics that your prospective partner is trying to conceal.

Astrologers are often asked to advise lovers involved in an ongoing relationship, or people who are contemplating a love affair. This important aspect of astrology is called synastry, and involves comparing the birth charts of the two people concerned. Each birth chart records the exact position of the planets at the moment and place of a person's birth.

By interpreting each chart separately, then comparing them, an astrologer can assess the compatibility of any two people, showing where problems may arise in their relationship, and where strong bonds will form.

One of the greatest astrological myths is that people of some signs are not compatible with people of certain other signs. This is completely untrue. Whatever your Sun sign, you can have a happy relationship with a person of any other sign.

YOU & YOUR LOVER

KNOWING ABOUT YOURSELF AND YOUR LOVER IS THE KEY TO
A HAPPY RELATIONSHIP. HERE WE REVEAL THE TRADITIONAL
ASSOCIATIONS OF PISCES, YOUR COMPATIBILITY WITH ALL THE
SUN SIGNS, AND THE FLOWERS LINKED WITH EACH SIGN.

ALL TREES THAT GROW
NEAR WATER, SUCH AS
THE WILLOW, ARE
TRADITIONALLY
ASSOCIATED
WITH PISCES

THE COLOR
ASSOCIATED
WITH PISCES
IS A MUTED
SEA GREEN

PISCEANS HAVE
COMPACT, WELL-
BUILT BODIES,
BUT MAY HAVE
TO WORK HARD
TO CONTROL
THEIR WEIGHT

THE PLANET
NEPTUNE,
WHICH HAS
THE NAME OF
THE ROMAN
GOD OF THE
SEA, RULES
PISCES

ALL FISH ARE
RULED BY PISCES,
AS ARE ANY
MAMMALS THAT
LIVE IN OR
NEAR THE
WATER

AS PISCES IS A WATER
SIGN, THE MAJORITY
OF PISCEANS LIKE TO
LIVE NEAR WATER

PISCES AND ARIES

The lively vigor of Aries may intimidate a dreamy Piscean. However, if you use your gentle charms to calm a fiery Arien, this combination could lead to a contented and rewarding union.

Lavender is a Geminian flower

Thistles are ruled by Aries

PISCES AND GEMINI

A restless Geminian may seem heartless to an emotional Piscean. Flighty Geminians can even indulge in infidelity. Both of you must moderate your behavior if your alliance is to succeed.

PISCES AND TAURUS

The warm passions of Taurus will boost your confidence, and your romantic charms will bring out the Taurean protective streak. This match is guaranteed to bring out the best in both of you.

The lily, and other white flowers, are ruled by Cancer

The rose is associated with Taurus

PISCES AND CANCER

You are both emotional water signs and are very compatible. This relationship will possess an aura of dreamy romance, and the two of you should enjoy a blissfully happy relationship.

PISCES AND LEO

Although you are very different creatures, you are both romantic daydreamers with a creative streak. You are quite happy for Leo to be the center of attention, so there will be no clash of egos.

Hydrangeas are governed by Libra

Sunflowers are ruled by Leo

PISCES AND LIBRA

Libra, like Pisces, is a romantic and considerate sign, and you will both try very hard to make and keep each other happy. This will be a supportive, loving, and sympathetic union.

PISCES AND VIRGO

Virgo and Pisces are opposite signs of the zodiac, and are very compatible. Virgos will keep you happy and secure, and you will delight them with your sense of poetry and romance.

Honeysuckle is attributed to Scorpio

Small, brightly colored flowers are associated with Virgo

PISCES AND SCORPIO

A gentle, dreamy Piscean could be intimidated by the intensity and power of Scorpio passion. Try to stand up for yourself and assert your personality, or a Scorpio may walk all over you.

– YOU & YOUR LOVER –

PISCES AND SAGITTARIUS
If you become overemotional, a carefree, footloose Sagittarian will simply gallop off into the distance and abandon you. Sagittarian optimism and cheerfulness will liven you up.

Carnations are ruled by Sagittarius

PISCES AND CAPRICORN
The will to succeed drives Capricorns, and their determination to win will not appeal to you. However, their reliability and solidity should make you feel very secure.

Pansies are Capricorn flowers

Orchids are associated with Aquarius

PISCES AND AQUARIUS
Your Piscean emotions may overwhelm freedom-loving Aquarians. If you can understand that they need their own space, this has the potential to be a very loving and fulfilling match.

Viburnum is governed by Pisces

PISCES AND PISCES
Pisceans need a decisive and determined partner to help them reach their full potential. To make this match work, the pair of you must learn to be a little more organized and assertive.

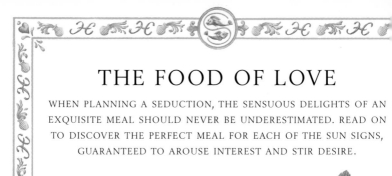

THE FOOD OF LOVE

WHEN PLANNING A SEDUCTION, THE SENSUOUS DELIGHTS OF AN
EXQUISITE MEAL SHOULD NEVER BE UNDERESTIMATED. READ ON
TO DISCOVER THE PERFECT MEAL FOR EACH OF THE SUN SIGNS,
GUARANTEED TO AROUSE INTEREST AND STIR DESIRE.

*Pisceans will
find the subtle
and delicate flavor
of melon sorbet
particularly
appetizing.*

– THE FOOD OF LOVE –

FOR ARIENS
Spicy mulligatawny soup
·
Peppered steak
·
Baked Alaska

FOR TAUREANS
Cream of cauliflower soup
·
Tournedos Rossini
·
Rich chocolate and brandy mousse

FOR GEMINIANS
Seafood and avocado salad
·
Piquant stir-fried pork with ginger
·
Zabaglione

FOR CANCERIANS
Artichoke vinaigrette
·
Sole Bonne Femme
·
Almond soufflé

– THE FOOD OF LOVE –

FOR LEOS

Roasted tomato and garlic soup
·
Boeuf Stroganoff
·
Pears cooked in wine

FOR VIRGOS

Eggplant salad
·
Paella
·
French apple tart

FOR LIBRANS

Asparagus with hollandaise sauce
·
Pork with roasted apples
·
Strawberry Pavlova

FOR SCORPIOS

Vichyssoise
·
Lobster Newburg
·
Blueberry cream

– THE FOOD OF LOVE –

FOR SAGITTARIANS
Chilled cucumber soup
·
Nutty onion flan
·
Rhubarb crumble with fresh cream

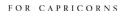

FOR CAPRICORNS
Eggs Florentine
·
Pork tenderloin stuffed with sage
·
Pineapple Pavlova

FOR AQUARIANS
Watercress soup
·
Chicken cooked with chili and lime
·
Lemon soufflé

FOR PISCEANS
French onion soup
·
Trout au vin rosé
·
Melon sorbet

PLACES TO LOVE

ONCE YOU HAVE WON YOUR LOVER'S HEART, A ROMANTIC
VACATION TOGETHER WILL SEAL YOUR LOVE. HERE, YOU
CAN DISCOVER THE PERFECT DESTINATION FOR EACH SUN
SIGN, FROM HISTORIC CITIES TO IDYLLIC BEACHES.

THE
EIFFEL
TOWER,
PARIS

ARIES

*Florence is an Arien
city, and its perfectly
preserved Renaissance
palaces and churches
will set the scene for
wonderful romance.*

TAURUS

*The unspoiled scenery
and unhurried pace
of life in rural Ireland
is sure to appeal to
patient and placid
Taureans.*

GEMINI

*Vivacious and restless
Geminians will feel at
home in the fast-paced
and sophisticated
atmosphere of
New York.*

CANCER

*The watery beauty
and uniquely romantic
atmosphere of Venice
is guaranteed to arouse
passion and stir the
Cancerian imagination.*

ST. BASIL'S
CATHEDRAL,
MOSCOW

AYERS ROCK/ULURU,
AUSTRALIA

LEO

Leos will fall in love all over again when surrounded by the picturesque charm and unspoiled medieval atmosphere of Prague.

VIRGO

Perhaps the most elegant and romantic of all cities, Paris is certainly the ideal setting for a stylish and fastidious Virgo.

LIBRA

The dramatic and exotic beauty of Upper Egypt and the Nile will provide the perfect backdrop for wooing a romantic Libran.

SCORPIO

Intense and passionate Scorpios will be strongly attracted by the whiff of danger present in the exotic atmosphere of New Orleans.

SAGITTARIUS

The wide-ranging spaces of the Australian outback will appeal to the Sagittarian love of freedom and the great outdoors.

CAPRICORN

Capricorns will be fascinated and inspired by the great historical monuments of Moscow, the most powerful of all Russian cities.

AQUARIUS

Intrepid Aquarians will be enthralled and amazed by the unusual sights and spectacular landscapes of the Indian subcontinent.

PISCES

Water-loving Pisceans will be at their most relaxed and romantic by the sea, perhaps on a small and unspoiled Mediterranean island.

THE PYRAMIDS, EGYPT

GONDOLAS, VENICE

THE TAJ MAHAL, INDIA

VENUS & MARS

LUCID, SHINING VENUS AND FIERY, RED MARS HAVE ALWAYS BEEN
ASSOCIATED WITH HUMAN LOVE AND PASSION. THE TWO
PLANETS HAVE A POWERFUL INFLUENCE ON OUR ATTITUDES
TOWARD LOVE, SEX, AND RELATIONSHIPS.

*T*he study of astrology
first began long before
humankind began to record
its own history. The earliest
astrological artifacts discovered,
scratches on bones recording the
phases of the Moon, date from
well before the invention of any
alphabet or writing system.

The planets Venus and Mars
have always been regarded as
having enormous significance
in astrology. This is evident from
the tentative attempts of early
astrologers to record the effects
of the two planets on humankind.
Hundreds of years later, the
positions of the planets were
carefully noted in personal
horoscopes. The earliest known
record is dated 410 BC: "Venus
[was] in the Bull, and Mars in
the Twins."

The bright, shining planet Venus
represents the gentle effect of
the soul on our physical lives.
It is responsible for a refined
and romantic sensuality – "pure"
love, untainted by sex. Venus
reigns over our attitudes toward
romance and the spiritual
dimension of love.

The planet Mars affects the
physical aspects of our lives –
our strength, both physical
and mental; our endurance; and
our ability to fight for survival.
Mars is also strongly linked to
the sex drive of both men and
women. Mars governs our
physical energy, sexuality, and
levels of desire.

Venus is known as an
"inferior" planet, because its
orbit falls between Earth and
the Sun. Venus orbits the Sun

LOVE CONQUERS ALL

In Botticelli's Venus and Mars, *the warlike, fiery energy of Mars, the god of war, has been overcome by the gentle charms of Venus, the goddess of love.*

closely, and its position in the zodiac is always in a sign near that of the Sun. As a result, the planet can only have occupied one of five given signs at the time of your birth – your Sun sign, or the two signs before or after it. For example, if you were born with the Sun in Virgo, Venus can only have occupied Cancer, Leo, Virgo, Libra, or Scorpio at that moment.

Mars, on the other hand, is a "superior" planet. Its orbit lies on the other side of Earth from the Sun, and therefore the planet may have occupied any of the 12 signs at the moment of your birth.

On the following pages (24–45) we provide you with fascinating insights into how Mars and Venus govern your attitudes toward love, sex, and relationships. To ascertain which sign of the zodiac the planets occupied at the moment of your birth, you must first consult the tables on pages 52–61. Then turn to page 24 and read on.

YOUR LOVE LIFE

THE PLANET VENUS REPRESENTS LOVE, HARMONY, AND UNITY.
WORK OUT WHICH SIGN OF THE ZODIAC VENUS OCCUPIED AT
THE MOMENT OF YOUR BIRTH (SEE PAGES 52–57), AND READ ON.

VENUS IN CAPRICORN

From Capricorn, Venus will help to curb the powerful waves of Piscean passion that continually wash over you. When you fall in love, this restraining influence will prove extremely beneficial. Venus in Capricorn will not lessen your ability to have fun or make you less affectionate, but it will bring a practical aspect to your personality that your fellow Pisceans may envy.

From this sign, Venus will play the part of a gentle yet practical friend, bringing you a strong streak of Capricorn caution and common sense. Your powerful and changeable emotions will be easier to control, and you are less likely to pledge yourself forever

on the basis of a brief spark of attraction. Instead, you will choose your lover very carefully and thoughtfully.

When Venus shines from Capricorn, material status will be very important to you. When you look around for a potential long-term partner, you may choose someone for the wrong reasons – perhaps because he or she is particularly attractive, intelligent, or wealthy. You may regard your lover as a trophy that you have won, exciting envy and admiration in others. Do not allow worldly ambition to encourage you to pick a lover for the wrong reasons – such a partnership will not be built on a solid foundation and is unlikely to enjoy lasting success.

Venus in Capricorn emphasizes duty and diligence, and you will work hard for your family. You enjoy the role of provider, and will want your family life to be secure both financially and emotionally. As a result, you may gradually find yourself working longer and longer hours, reducing the amount of time you can spend with your partner and family. Do not neglect your domestic life. Try to spend your time as sensibly as you spend your money, and divide your time and energy equally between your work and your home life.

All Pisceans have a generous amount of love and affection to lavish on their fortunate partner, and you have the ability to combine that love with a valuable element of common sense. As a result, you will make a warmhearted, passionate, and supportive partner.

VENUS IN AQUARIUS

*W*hen Venus shines from Aquarius, the planet will imbue you with an enigmatic allure and an indefinable air of glamor. You are likely to be surrounded by a throng of admirers, and will revel in the attention they lavish upon you.

You will enjoy all this admiration and attention. However, due to the independent, freedom-loving influence of Aquarius, you may be somewhat apprehensive when a friend or lover indicates a desire to move your relationship onto a more serious level. When Venus occupies Aquarius, you will be essentially a free spirit. If asked to make a long-term commitment you may experience an uncharacteristic urge to beat a hasty retreat or even slump into a depression as you realize just how much your privacy and independence will be curtailed by a permanent partnership. In such a situation, you must draw on all your Piscean romanticism and tenderness, fighting off any Aquarian reluctance to make a serious commitment.

The cool restraint brought by Venus in Aquarius will be very useful, because it will help you to regulate the intensity and passion of your Piscean emotions. You will find it easier to control your powerful feelings and to assume a more rational outlook on life. The Aquarian influence will also bring you a valuable infusion of practical common sense combined with a keen sense of intuition.

People born under this planetary placing tend to be attracted by lovely things and beautiful people. Appearances can sometimes assume too much importance for you. It is not wise to select a partner on the basis of looks alone – your

relationship must be built on sturdier foundations. Friendship and understanding will endure forever, whereas the appeal of beauty will eventually fade.

Because of the kindness of Pisces and the loyalty of Aquarius, you will be a faithful and constant friend, always ready with moral support and a sympathetic ear. However, Pisceans often have a perverse streak, and you may find that you resist fitting in with the wishes of others. Despite this trait, your kindness and generosity ensure that you are a popular and valued companion.

The combination of your innate Piscean tenderness and romance with the Aquarian sparkle and glamor is irresistible. Due to this planetary placing, you are guaranteed to be an extremely sought-after and seductive lover.

VENUS IN PISCES

*A*ccording to astrological tradition, Venus is very harmoniously and happily placed in Pisces. However, when the Sun and Venus both occupy this sign, the powerful influence of Pisces will need careful control.

Pisceans tend to fall in love very easily. You are extremely trusting and openhearted, and almost anyone who sets out to win you over will easily succeed. You should be aware that your abundance of Piscean emotions may quite unexpectedly run away with you. As a result, you may find yourself making rash and generous sacrifices for your partner. Pisceans have an inclination to idolize their lovers, and tend to regard them in the flattering glow of rose-colored glasses. You may even treat your partner in such a devoted and adoring fashion that he or she begins to take you for granted and eventually treats you like a doormat. If your partner turns out to be selfish or inconsiderate, there is a danger that your kindhearted and altruistic nature might be ruthlessly exploited.

Pisceans are so idealistic when it comes to affairs of the heart that they do not always learn by their mistakes. If you manage to extricate yourself from an unhappy relationship or a self-obsessed and uncaring lover, you are likely to fall head over heels in love two weeks later, and may be well on the way to experiencing the same heartbreak all over again. You must strive to adopt a more cautious and judicious attitude when searching for a lover. Before committing yourself, consider how compatible you and your potential partner are. Once you are involved, be ready to acknowledge his or her character flaws that may come to light.

Dreamy, poetic Pisceans have an amazing ability to avoid facing facts, which can be very difficult if their relationships enter into troubled waters. You have a tendency to take the easy way out of emotional upsets by pretending that nothing is wrong, which is not a very constructive solution to problems within your relationship. Try to cultivate a little less emotion and a little more common sense.

Pisceans can sometimes bowl over a potential partner with their ardor and romanticism. When you meet someone you are attracted to, you must not feel rebuffed if he or she is not quite as responsive and enthusiastic as you, because not everybody is so open with feelings. From Venus, Pisces can bring a tendency towards self-doubt. Do not underestimate your powers of attraction.

VENUS IN ARIES

*T*he watery and sensitive emotions of Pisces will be transformed by the fiery and ardent influence of Venus in Aries. You will be caring and tender, but at the same time vigorous and enthusiastic. However, your powerful Piscean emotions will still dominate your personality and will gush out in a torrent when you meet someone you find attractive.

You may discover that Arien determination and forcefulness clash with your Piscean lack of confidence. Due to the bold and impetuous influence of Venus in Aries, when you are attracted to someone your instinct will be to pursue him or her openly and eagerly. However, an element of Piscean self-doubt could dampen your eagerness and enthusiasm, and you may be reluctant to make your feelings obvious. Employ all your Arien dynamism and courage to overcome any insecurities, and allow the warm and enthusiastic aspects of your personality to come to the fore.

With this placing, Piscean romanticism is likely to combine with Arien impetuosity. When you fall in love, you will regard each new liaison as the great passion of your life, throwing yourself headlong into the relationship. This may not always be the wisest approach to adopt, because if your alliance does not succeed you will be disillusioned and saddened. Try not to be too impulsive and reckless – instead try to cultivate the valuable qualities of caution and prudence.

You will be a generous partner, happy to lavish both money and emotion on your partner. Generosity is highly attractive, but your openhanded attitude toward money may lead you into financial difficulties.

Pisceans tend to be easygoing and compliant, happy to go along with the wishes of their friends and lovers. However, when Venus shines from Aries, a most uncharacteristic streak of selfishness could manifest itself in your personality. A ruthless determination to always get your own way is not an attractive attribute; therefore, be alert to any self-indulgence or self-absorption.

The gentle and considerate Piscean elements in your personality should help diminish any selfish urges.

If you are able to combine the valuable strength and energy of Venus in Aries with your innate Piscean gentleness and sensuality, you will make a considerate yet dynamic partner, and will find it easy to form an extremely happy, long-lasting, and successful relationship.

VENUS IN TAURUS

*T*n astrological terms, Venus "rules" Taurus, and therefore the planet will work very powerfully for you. From Taurus, the influence of Venus is loving and tender, and you will do everything in your power to keep your lover contented and fulfilled. As a lover, you will be extremely generous and altruistic, and will lavish attention on your fortunate partner.

Pisceans are often extremely emotional types, and when they fall for someone, they fall head over heels, and without restraint. This recklessness can lead to heartbreak and disillusionment. Luckily, from Taurus, Venus will provide a more cautious and levelheaded influence. You are less likely than many Pisceans to throw yourself fervently into an affair, and will be quite happy to approach a new relationship slowly and steadily, feeling that there is no need to rush.

Pisceans are intensely romantic, and you will revel in the heady atmosphere of romance and excitement that pervades the early stages of a relationship. Your courtship and seduction will be characterized by luxury. You are likely to have a true Taurean appreciation of the good things in life – delicious food, fine wines, and comfortable and elegant surroundings. Venus in Taurus often brings with it a love of rich food; therefore, you may have to struggle to keep your weight down.

From Taurus, the influence of Venus could make you rather possessive – a trait that your partner may find difficult to tolerate. Fortunately, Venus will make you more practical and emotionally stable than some Pisceans, and will bring you a generous helping of common sense. This should enable you to recognize any

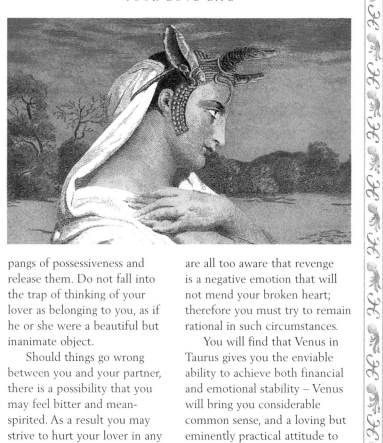

pangs of possessiveness and release them. Do not fall into the trap of thinking of your lover as belonging to you, as if he or she were a beautiful but inanimate object.

Should things go wrong between you and your partner, there is a possibility that you may feel bitter and mean-spirited. As a result you may strive to hurt your lover in any way possible. Deep down, you

are all too aware that revenge is a negative emotion that will not mend your broken heart; therefore you must try to remain rational in such circumstances.

You will find that Venus in Taurus gives you the enviable ability to achieve both financial and emotional stability – Venus will bring you considerable common sense, and a loving but eminently practical attitude to both love and money.

YOUR SEX LIFE

THE PLANET MARS REPRESENTS PHYSICAL AND SEXUAL ENERGY.
WORK OUT WHICH SIGN OF THE ZODIAC MARS OCCUPIED AT THE
MOMENT OF YOUR BIRTH (SEE PAGES 58–61), AND READ ON.

MARS IN ARIES

*W*hen Mars shines from Aries, you will possess a high level of physical energy, which will increase both your sex drive and your level of emotional passion.

You will be an ardent and rewarding lover, because the fiery passion of Aries will complement the romantic ardor of the typical Piscean. Arien energy and enthusiasm will overcome any Piscean lack of confidence, and you will be more assertive than many of your fellow Pisceans.

Any Piscean propensity to self-deception will be lessened by Mars in Aries, and you will be a forthright and honest lover, scorning deceit and insincerity.

MARS IN TAURUS

*F*rom Taurus, Mars will bring you a degree of sexual passion that will rival your Piscean emotional resources in its intensity. As a result, you will be an extremely sensual and affectionate lover.

Due to the influence of Taurus, you will have greater physical stamina than many Pisceans, spiced with a touch of stubbornness. Taurean tenacity will make you very determined – once you have set your heart on a goal, you will do your utmost

to achieve it. This applies to potential lovers as well as ambitions or material possessions.

The Taurean influence is usually a placid one, and this placing should have a steadying effect on your volatile emotions. When upset, Pisceans are more likely to burst into tears than to throw dishes, but you may possess a hot temper. This will lie dormant for much of the time but, when your anger flares up, the resulting scene will be an extremely stormy one.

MARS IN GEMINI

This placing of Mars will heighten your sexual appetite. You will throw yourself with enthusiasm into the sexual side of your relationship, and will be eager to experiment. The adventurous Geminian attitude toward sex will combine with Piscean passion and eroticism. As a result, your lovemaking will be seductive and imaginative.

When Mars is in Gemini, you will thrive on novelty and change. Gemini is the sign of duality, and Pisceans tend to be a little deceptive. Resist the temptation to become involved in illicit affairs. You must not allow a yearning for excitement to endanger a happy and secure relationship. Luckily, you will find it easy to discuss any problems with your partner, and you are likely to be articulate and eloquent.

You will be a vigorous and athletic lover with plenty of stamina and, of all the Sun signs, are most likely to remain sexually active well into old age.

MARS IN CANCER

*P*isceans are renowned for their tender and romantic approach to love, and the influence of Cancer will make you even more sensual and caring. Your lovemaking will be passionate yet tender, and you will be an extremely seductive and imaginative lover.

You will have an instinctive awareness of your partner's needs and desires, and will work hard to ensure that he or she is satisfied and fulfilled. There is a danger that you could be almost too devoted, making your lover feel claustrophobic. Bear in mind the force of your emotions – if they are strongly focused on your lover, your feelings could be overwhelming in their intensity.

Pisceans are usually sweet-natured and easygoing, but from Cancer Mars may make you a little touchy. In the heat of an argument, you may make hurtful comments. Try to control your sharp tongue, or you could find that it makes trouble between you and your lover.

MARS IN LEO

From Leo, Mars will bring you a great zest for life, coupled with a determination that your friends and lover should enjoy themselves as much as you. This concern for the happiness of others extends to your sex life, and ensures that you will be a considerate and generous lover.

The influence of Mars from Leo will make you a natural leader – resourceful, determined, and energetic. Leonine vitality and dynamism will soon overcome any Piscean lack of confidence or self-doubt. When you meet a potential partner you will pursue your quarry forcefully and boldly, and will employ all the seductive charm Mars brings from Leo to win the heart of your prospective lover.

You have a hot temper, which tends to flare up suddenly and unexpectedly. Try to resist the temptation to cause a scene. Happily, your anger will die down as quickly as it bubbles up, and you will soon be eager to kiss and make up with your lover.

MARS IN VIRGO

The uncontrolled torrent of Piscean emotion may be checked by the cool influence of Mars from Virgo, but do not allow the sign to repress your warm Piscean sensuality. If you can allow the passion of Pisces to develop the earthy sensuality of Virgo, you will be a rewarding and passionate lover.

Pisceans tend to be very impulsive, throwing themselves into relationships without a great deal of forethought. If their alliance does not succeed, they often become disillusioned and depressed. However, Mars in Virgo will provide a cautious and practical influence. You will be more self-controlled when it comes to forming relationships, and less likely to fling yourself into a disastrous liaison.

You are a dutiful and hard-working lover, and will labor with all the Virgoan diligence and Piscean emotional energy you possess to ensure that your relationship is fulfilling, harmonious, and long-lasting.

MARS IN LIBRA

When Mars shines from Libra, you will want to enjoy a passionate and sensuous sex life within the secure confines of a harmonious and long-lasting relationship. Due to the Libran influence, you may be a little languid, and the prospect of energetic sex will not always appeal. You must overcome your laziness, because once aroused you are an ardent, skillful lover.

You will work hard to achieve a happy and sexually fulfilling relationship, but do not become obsequious in your attempts to keep your lover content. There is a danger that such an attitude may become cloying and claustrophobic.

Although Libra tends to dampen the energy of Mars, the planet may encourage you to argue with your lover. The Libran influence is generally a peaceful one, but when it comes to romantic relationships, you may cause quarrels simply because you so enjoy the ritual of kissing and making up.

– YOUR SEX LIFE –

MARS IN SCORPIO

From Scorpio, the Martian influence is very powerful, and will increase your sex drive. Your lovemaking will be energetic, passionate, and erotically charged.

As a result, it is essential that you find a partner who possesses a similarly high libido. A romantic and sensual sex life is important to all Pisceans; due to the influence of Scorpio you may become very frustrated and irritable if you do not enjoy frequent and satisfying sex.

Pisceans tend to be gentle and considerate lovers, but when Mars shines from Scorpio, you may find that jealousy rears its ugly head. You may become possessive, filled with a black rage if your partner pays any attention to someone else. As your emotions are strong, any jealousy will be very evident, and could create an oppressive atmosphere within your relationship. You must draw on all your Piscean kindness and sensitivity to overcome this destructive emotion.

MARS IN SAGITTARIUS

When Mars shines from Sagittarius, the planet will fill you with energy and zest for life. You will be more active and adventurous than many Pisceans. As a result, your sex life will be dynamic, imaginative, and exciting.

This planetary placing suggests that you will thrive on constant challenge and novelty, and a partner who can stimulate your mind and equal your sex drive will be a perfect match for you. If you are not mentally and physically fulfilled by your partner, you may become restless and could even turn to illicit affairs to provide a spark of excitement.

Pisceans tend to be very selfless, and happy to comply with the wishes of others. However, the Sagittarian influence will make you more assertive and less malleable. This is a beneficial influence, because it should prevent you from adopting a submissive role within your relationship.

MARS IN CAPRICORN

*T*he placing of Mars in Capricorn can be very beneficial for a Piscean. The cool and restrained Capricorn influence will steady your rather volatile emotions and impart a valuable degree of self-control and discipline.

When Mars shines from Capricorn, you are unlikely to be an uncontrollably passionate lover. However, you will possess a consistently strong sex drive and plenty of stamina. Capricorns aim to excel at everything they turn their attention toward. Therefore, when Mars occupies this sign your lovemaking will be skilled and expert.

Due to the Capricorn influence from Mars, you will be ambitious and determined. Once you have set your sights on a potential lover, you will not rest until you have won his or her heart. A degree of Capricorn forcefulness and determination will make a valuable addition to your easygoing Piscean personality.

MARS IN AQUARIUS

From Aquarius, Mars may lessen the strength of your emotions. This will only work to your advantage, because your powerful Piscean feelings can so easily run away with you. You will possess more self-control than the majority of Pisceans and will be less likely to burst into tears or throw a tantrum.

Aquarius tends to bring a rather remote and detached influence from Mars, but despite this you will still possess a strong and steady sex drive. Pisceans are passionate and imaginative lovers, and your sex life will be active and inventive.

Mars in Aquarius will bring you a love of independence, and you will demand a degree of freedom within your relationship. This placing is likely to bring you a decidedly unconventional streak, and you may find that you are stubbornly determined to have your own way. Try not to become too eccentric, or potential suitors may be intimidated by your unorthodox behavior.

MARS IN PISCES

When Mars occupies Pisces with the Sun, your powerful emotional energy will be doubled. Your physical energy may not be very strong, but you will be an imaginative, passionate, and sensual lover.

Pisceans are extremely tenderhearted and romantic. When you fall in love, there is a danger that you may overwhelm your new lover with the force of your emotions. You must try not to overpower your partner with passionate demonstrations of your love, for your constant attentions may eventually create a somewhat claustrophobic and restrictive atmosphere.

When the Sun and Mars both shine from Pisces, you will be an idealistic and starry-eyed lover. You are likely to possess the typical Piscean tendency to place your lover on a pedestal. Try not to worship him or her too much, because you will be seriously disappointed when you eventually realize that your idol has feet of clay.

TOKENS OF LOVE

ASTROLOGY CAN GIVE YOU A FASCINATING INSIGHT INTO
YOUR LOVER'S PERSONALITY AND ATTITUDE TOWARD LOVE.
IT CAN ALSO PROVIDE YOU WITH SOME HELPFUL HINTS WHEN
YOU WANT TO CHOOSE THE PERFECT GIFT FOR YOUR LOVER.

INDIAN
HAIR
ORNAMENT

BELGIAN
CHOCOLATES

ARIES
*The head is the part
of the body ruled by
Aries, and unusual
hair products or
accessories
will make
an ideal
present.*

TAPESTRY
CUSHION

GEMINI
*Instead of chocolates,
buy your Geminian
lover Jordan almonds
or mixed nuts.*

JORDAN
ALMONDS

TAURUS
*A lavish and luxurious
cushion will enchant your
Taurean lover, as will rich
handmade chocolates.*

- TOKENS OF LOVE -

CANCER

Cancerians adore unusual curios and will also be delighted by luxurious soap. The pearl is the Cancerian gemstone, and pearl jewelry will be a meaningful gift.

BRASS BIRD
CURIO

DELICATELY
SCENTED
SOAP

LEO

Flamboyant Leos appreciate boldly colored, handcrafted objects. Gold is the Leo metal, and anything gold or golden-colored will have great appeal.

HANDMADE
BROOCH

PEARL
NECKLACE

GOLD
"COCKTAIL"
WRISTWATCH

REGENCY-
STYLE
WOODEN
CHAIR

VIRGO

Any objects made from wood will make the perfect gift for Virgos because they are drawn to natural materials.

– TOKENS OF LOVE –

WHITE
ROSES

LIBRA
Romantic Librans will
revel in seductive gifts
such as bouquets of
roses or silky lingerie.

SILK
LINGERIE

TABLE
LAMP

SCORPIO
A handsome lamp
is sure to be
proudly displayed
in a Scorpio home.

SAGITTARIUS
Adventurous Sagittarians
love to travel, and travel
books and accessories, such
as maps or compasses, will
be greatly appreciated.

TRAVEL
BOOKS

VICTORIAN
COMPASS

FOUNTAIN PEN

CAPRICORN

An old-fashioned fountain pen, elegant candles, or a glass decanter will all impress a fastidious Capricorn.

HEART-PATTERNED CANDLES

GIVING A BIRTHSTONE

The most personal gift you can give your lover is the gem linked to his or her Sun sign.

MOONSTONE

ARIES: *diamond*
TAURUS: *emerald*
GEMINI: *agate* • CANCER: *pearl*
LEO: *ruby* • VIRGO: *sardonyx*
LIBRA: *sapphire* • SCORPIO: *opal*
SAGITTARIUS: *topaz*
CAPRICORN: *amethyst*
AQUARIUS: *aquamarine*
PISCES: *moonstone*

HAND-BLOWN GLASS

WHITE ORCHID

AQUARIUS

Aquarians adore unusual and original gifts, such as hand-made modern glassware. If you are giving your Aquarian lover flowers, choose orchids.

PISCES

A sumptuous silk scarf will beguile a sensual Piscean. Iridescent glassware will also delight your Piscean lover.

THAI SILK SCARF

YOUR PERMANENT RELATIONSHIP

PISCEANS POUR THEIR PLENTIFUL SUPPLIES OF EMOTION INTO
THEIR PERMANENT RELATIONSHIPS. ROMANTIC AND SENTIMENTAL,
YOU WILL WORK HARD TO ACHIEVE A SUCCESSFUL PARTNERSHIP.

Tenderness and affection are the trademarks of a Piscean in love, and you will make a sympathetic and caring partner. You are prepared to work hard to ensure that your relationship is successful, happy, and long-lasting.

Pisceans have an unfortunate tendency to adopt a rather submissive role within their relationships – make sure that you do not repress your own wishes and opinions. Your submission could encourage your partner to become selfish, and you could find yourself always giving way to this person. Such adoring submission might initially be flattering, but your partner could eventually feel overwhelmed by your dependency. It is important that you retain a sense of your own identity and voice your own opinions, rather than always deferring to your partner.

Pisceans often have a high emotional level, which you should try to keep under control. This does not mean that you cannot occasionally allow your emotions free rein, but a continual storm of emotion can lead to needless confrontations. Pisceans can worry unduly about their lovers, largely because of their fertile imaginations. You may think that things are going terribly wrong with your relationship, when in fact all is entirely harmonious. Try to keep a logical perspective. Do not let your vivid imagination

A JOINT FUTURE
On a Sailing Ship, *by Caspar David Friedrich, shows a newly married couple sailing into a bright but unknown future together.*

run away with you – any lateness on the part of your lover is far more likely to be due to heavy traffic than to any great disaster or catastrophe.

If problems arise in your relationship, resist the typical Piscean habit of trying to wriggle out of accepting the blame. This behavior may worsen the situation. Try to own up to your misdemeanors rather than making excuses.

Pisceans hate to hurt others, and can economize with the truth in order to extricate themselves from a difficult situation, or to avoid hurting their lover's feelings. Resist the temptation to be evasive or vague. Talk any problems through – the ability to discuss your altercations honestly is one of the major ingredients of a successful relationship.

VENUS & MARS TABLES

THESE TABLES WILL ENABLE YOU TO DISCOVER WHICH SIGNS
VENUS AND MARS OCCUPIED AT THE MOMENT OF YOUR BIRTH.
TURN TO PAGES 24–45 TO INVESTIGATE THE QUALITIES OF THESE
SIGNS, AND TO FIND OUT HOW THEY WORK WITH YOUR SUN SIGN.

*T*he tables on pages 53–61
will enable you to discover
the positions of Venus and Mars at
the moment of your birth.

First find your year of birth
on the top line of the appropriate
table, then find your month of
birth in the left-hand column.
Where the column for your year
of birth intersects with the row
for your month of birth, you
will find a group of figures and
zodiacal glyphs. These figures
and glyphs show which sign of
the zodiac the planet occupied

on the first day of that month,
and any date during that month
on which the planet moved into
another sign.

For example, to ascertain the
position of Venus on May 10,
1968, run your finger down the
column marked 1968 until you
reach the row for May. The row
of numbers and glyphs shows
that Venus occupied Aries on
May 1, entered Taurus on May 4,
and then moved into Gemini on
May 28. Therefore, on May 10,
Venus was in Taurus.

---

*If you were born on a day when one of
the planets was moving into a new sign,
it may be impossible to determine your
Venus and Mars signs completely
accurately. If the characteristics described
on the relevant pages do not seem to
apply to you, read the interpretation of
the sign before and after. One of
these signs will be appropriate.*

ZODIACAL GLYPHS

♈	Aries	♌	Libra
♉	Taurus	♏	Scorpio
♊	Gemini	♐	Sagittarius
♋	Cancer	♑	Capricorn
♌	Leo	♒	Aquarius
♍	Virgo	♓	Pisces

– VENUS TABLES –

♀	1921	1922	1923	1924	1925	1926	1927	1928
JAN	1 ♒ 7 ♓	1 ♑ 25 ♒	1 ♏ 3 ♐	1 ♒ 20 ♓	1 ♐ 15 ♑	1 ♒	1 ♑ 10 ♒	1 ♏ 5 ♐ 30 ♑
FEB	1 ♓ 3 ♈	1 ♒ 18 ♓	1 ♐ 7 ♑	1 ♓ 14 ♈	1 ♑ 8 ♒	1 ♒	1 ♒ 3 ♓ 27 ♈	1 ♑ 23 ♒
MAR	1 ♈ 8 ♉	1 ♓ 14 ♈	1 ♑ 7 ♒	1 ♈ 10 ♉	1 ♒ 5 ♓ 29 ♈	1 ♒	1 ♈ 23 ♉	1 ♒ 19 ♓
APR	1 ♉ 26 ♈	1 ♈ 7 ♉	1 ♒ 2 ♓ 27 ♈	1 ♉ 6 ♊	1 ♈ 22 ♉	1 ♒ 26 ♓	1 ♉ 17 ♊	1 ♓ 12 ♈
MAY	1 ♈	1 ♉ 2 ♊ 26 ♋	1 ♈ 22 ♉	1 ♊ 7 ♋	1 ♉ 16 ♊	1 ♓ 7 ♈	1 ♊ 13 ♋	1 ♈ 7 ♉ 31 ♊
JUN	1 ♈ 3 ♉	1 ♋ 20 ♌	1 ♉ 16 ♊	1 ♋	1 ♊ 10 ♋	1 ♈ 3 ♉ 29 ♊	1 ♋ 9 ♌	1 ♊ 24 ♋
JUL	1 ♉ 9 ♊	1 ♌ 16 ♍	1 ♊ 11 ♋	1 ♋	1 ♋ 4 ♌ 29 ♍	1 ♊ 25 ♋	1 ♌ 8 ♍	1 ♋ 19 ♌
AUG	1 ♊ 6 ♋	1 ♍ 11 ♎	1 ♋ 4 ♌ 28 ♍	1 ♋	1 ♍ 23 ♎	1 ♋ 19 ♌	1 ♍	1 ♌ 12 ♍
SEP	1 ♌ 27 ♍	1 ♎ 8 ♏	1 ♍ 22 ♎	1 ♋ 8 ♌	1 ♎ 17 ♏	1 ♌ 12 ♍	1 ♍	1 ♍ 5 ♎ 30 ♏
OCT	1 ♍ 21 ♎	1 ♏ 11 ♐	1 ♎ 16 ♏	1 ♌ 8 ♍	1 ♏ 12 ♐	1 ♍ 6 ♎ 30 ♏	1 ♍	1 ♏ 24 ♐
NOV	1 ♎ 14 ♏	1 ♐ 29 ♏	1 ♏ 9 ♐	1 ♍ 3 ♎ 28 ♏	1 ♐ 7 ♑	1 ♏ 23 ♐	1 ♍ 10 ♎	1 ♐ 18 ♑
DEC	1 ♏ 8 ♐	1 ♏	1 ♐ 3 ♑ 27 ♒	1 ♏ 22 ♐	1 ♑ 6 ♒	1 ♐ 17 ♑	1 ♎ 9 ♏	1 ♑ 13 ♒

♀	1929	1930	1931	1932	1933	1934	1935	1936
JAN	1 ♒ 7 ♓	1 ♑ 25 ♒	1 ♏ 4 ♐	1 ♒ 20 ♓	1 ♐ 15 ♑	1 ♒	1 ♑ 9 ♒	1 ♏ 4 ♐ 29 ♑
FEB	1 ♓ 3 ♈	1 ♒ 17 ♓	1 ♐ 7 ♑	1 ♓ 13 ♈	1 ♑ 8 ♒	1 ♒	1 ♒ 2 ♓ 27 ♈	1 ♑ 23 ♒
MAR	1 ♈ 9 ♉	1 ♓ 13 ♈	1 ♑ 6 ♒	1 ♈ 10 ♉	1 ♒ 4 ♓ 28 ♈	1 ♒	1 ♈ 23 ♉	1 ♒ 18 ♓
APR	1 ♉ 21 ♈	1 ♈ 7 ♉	1 ♓ 27 ♈	1 ♉ 6 ♊	1 ♈ 21 ♉	1 ♒ 26 ♓	1 ♉ 17 ♊	1 ♓ 12 ♈
MAY	1 ♈	1 ♊ 26 ♋	1 ♈ 22 ♉	1 ♊ 7 ♋	1 ♉ 16 ♊	1 ♓ 7 ♈	1 ♊ 12 ♋	1 ♈ 6 ♉ 30 ♊
JUN	1 ♈ 4 ♉	1 ♋ 20 ♌	1 ♉ 15 ♊	1 ♋	1 ♊ 9 ♋	1 ♈ 3 ♉ 29 ♊	1 ♋ 8 ♌	1 ♊ 24 ♋
JUL	1 ♉ 9 ♊	1 ♌ 15 ♍	1 ♊ 10 ♋	1 ♋ 14 ♊ 29 ♋	1 ♋ 4 ♌ 28 ♍	1 ♊ 24 ♋	1 ♌ 8 ♍	1 ♋ 18 ♌
AUG	1 ♊ 6 ♋	1 ♍ 11 ♎	1 ♋ 4 ♌ 28 ♍	1 ♋	1 ♍ 22 ♎	1 ♋ 18 ♌	1 ♍	1 ♌ 12 ♍
SEP	1 ♌ 26 ♍	1 ♎ 8 ♏	1 ♍ 21 ♎	1 ♋ 9 ♌	1 ♎ 16 ♏	1 ♌ 12 ♍	1 ♍	1 ♍ 5 ♎ 29 ♏
OCT	1 ♍ 21 ♎	1 ♏ 13 ♐	1 ♎ 15 ♏	1 ♌ 8 ♍	1 ♏ 12 ♐	1 ♍ 6 ♎ 30 ♏	1 ♍	1 ♏ 24 ♐
NOV	1 ♎ 14 ♏	1 ♐ 23 ♏	1 ♏ 8 ♐	1 ♍ 3 ♎ 28 ♏	1 ♐ 7 ♑	1 ♏ 23 ♐	1 ♍ 10 ♎	1 ♐ 17 ♑
DEC	1 ♏ 8 ♐ 31 ♑	1 ♏	1 ♐ 2 ♑ 26 ♒	1 ♏ 22 ♐	1 ♑ 6 ♒	1 ♐ 17 ♑	1 ♎ 9 ♏	1 ♑ 12 ♒

♀	1937	1938	1939	1940	1941	1942	1943	1944
JAN	1 ♒ 7 ♓	1 ♑ 24 ♒	1 ♏ 5 ♐	1 ♒ 19 ♓	1 ♐ 14 ♑	1 ♒	1 ♑ 9 ♒	1 ♏ 4 ♐ 29 ♑
FEB	1 ♓ 3 ♈	1 ♒ 17 ♓	1 ♐ 7 ♑	1 ♓ 13 ♈	1 ♑ 7 ♒	1 ♒	1 ♒ 2 ♓ 26 ♈	1 ♑ 22 ♒
MAR	1 ♈ 10 ♉	1 ♓ 13 ♈	1 ♑ 6 ♒	1 ♈ 9 ♉	1 ♒ 3 ♓ 28 ♈	1 ♒	1 ♈ 22 ♉	1 ♒ 18 ♓
APR	1 ♉ 15 ♈	1 ♈ 6 ♉ 30 ♊	1 ♓ 26 ♈	1 ♉ 5 ♊	1 ♈ 21 ♉	1 ♒ 7 ♓	1 ♉ 16 ♊	1 ♓ 11 ♈
MAY	1 ♈	1 ♊ 25 ♋	1 ♈ 21 ♉	1 ♊ 25 ♋	1 ♉ 15 ♊	1 ♓ 7 ♈	1 ♊ 12 ♋	1 ♈ 5 ♉ 30 ♊
JUN	1 ♈ 5 ♉	1 ♋ 19 ♌	1 ♉ 15 ♊	1 ♋	1 ♊ 8 ♋	1 ♈ 3 ♉ 28 ♊	1 ♋ 8 ♌	1 ♊ 23 ♋
JUL	1 ♉ 8 ♊	1 ♌ 15 ♍	1 ♊ 10 ♋	1 ♋ 6 ♊	1 ♋ 3 ♌ 28 ♍	1 ♊ 24 ♋	1 ♌ 8 ♍	1 ♋ 18 ♌
AUG	1 ♊ 5 ♋	1 ♍ 10 ♎	1 ♋ 3 ♌ 27 ♍	1 ♊ 2 ♋	1 ♍ 22 ♎	1 ♋ 18 ♌	1 ♍	1 ♌ 11 ♍
SEP	1 ♌ 26 ♍	1 ♎ 8 ♏	1 ♍ 21 ♎	1 ♋ 9 ♌	1 ♎ 16 ♏	1 ♌ 11 ♍	1 ♍	1 ♍ 4 ♎ 29 ♏
OCT	1 ♍ 20 ♎	1 ♏ 14 ♐	1 ♎ 15 ♏	1 ♌ 7 ♍	1 ♏ 11 ♐	1 ♍ 5 ♎ 29 ♏	1 ♍	1 ♏ 23 ♐
NOV	1 ♎ 13 ♏	1 ♐ 16 ♏	1 ♏ 8 ♐	1 ♍ 2 ♎ 27 ♏	1 ♐ 7 ♑	1 ♏ 22 ♐	1 ♍ 10 ♎	1 ♐ 16 ♑
DEC	1 ♏ 7 ♐ 31 ♑	1 ♏	1 ♐ 2 ♑ 26 ♒	1 ♏ 21 ♐	1 ♑ 6 ♒	1 ♐ 16 ♑	1 ♎ 9 ♏	1 ♑ 12 ♒

♀	1945	1946	1947	1948	1949	1950	1951	1952
JAN	1 ♒ 6 ♓	1 ♑ 23 ♒	1 ♏ 6 ♐	1 ♒ 19 ♓	1 ♐ 14 ♑	1 ♒	1 ♑ 8 ♒	1 ♏ 3 ♐ 28 ♑
FEB	1 ♓ 3 ♈	1 ♒ 16 ♓	1 ♐ 7 ♑	1 ♓ 12 ♈	1 ♑ 7 ♒	1 ♒	1 ♓ 25 ♈	1 ♑ 21 ♒
MAR	1 ♈ 12 ♉	1 ♓ 17 ♈	1 ♑ 6 ♒ 31 ♓	1 ♈ 9 ♉	1 ♒ 3 ♓ 27 ♈	1 ♒	1 ♈ 22 ♉	1 ♒ 17 ♓
APR	1 ♉ 8 ♈	1 ♈ 6 ♉ 30 ♊	1 ♓ 26 ♈	1 ♉ 5 ♊	1 ♈ 20 ♉	1 ♒ 6 ♓	1 ♉ 16 ♊	1 ♓ 10 ♈
MAY	1 ♈	1 ♊ 25 ♋	1 ♈ 21 ♉	1 ♊ 25 ♋	1 ♉ 15 ♊	1 ♓ 6 ♈	1 ♊ 12 ♋	1 ♈ 5 ♉ 29 ♊
JUN	1 ♈ 5 ♉	1 ♋ 19 ♌	1 ♉ 14 ♊	1 ♋	1 ♊ 8 ♋	1 ♈ 2 ♉ 28 ♊	1 ♋ 8 ♌	1 ♊ 23 ♋
JUL	1 ♉ 8 ♊	1 ♌ 14 ♍	1 ♊ 9 ♋	1 ♋ 6 ♊	1 ♋ 2 ♌ 27 ♍	1 ♊ 23 ♋	1 ♌ 9 ♍	1 ♋ 17 ♌
AUG	1 ♊ 5 ♋ 31 ♌	1 ♍ 10 ♎	1 ♋ 3 ♌ 27 ♍	1 ♊ 2 ♋	1 ♍ 21 ♎	1 ♋ 18 ♌	1 ♍	1 ♌ 10 ♍
SEP	1 ♌ 25 ♍	1 ♎ 8 ♏	1 ♍ 20 ♎	1 ♋ 9 ♌	1 ♎ 15 ♏	1 ♌ 11 ♍	1 ♍	1 ♍ 4 ♎ 28 ♏
OCT	1 ♍ 20 ♎	1 ♏ 17 ♐	1 ♎ 14 ♏	1 ♌ 7 ♍	1 ♏ 11 ♐	1 ♍ 5 ♎ 29 ♏	1 ♍	1 ♏ 23 ♐
NOV	1 ♎ 13 ♏	1 ♐ 9 ♏	1 ♏ 7 ♐	1 ♍ 2 ♎ 27 ♏	1 ♐ 7 ♑	1 ♏ 22 ♐	1 ♍ 10 ♎	1 ♐ 16 ♑
DEC	1 ♏ 7 ♐ 31 ♑	1 ♏	1 ♑ 25 ♒	1 ♏ 21 ♐	1 ♑ 7 ♒	1 ♐ 15 ♑	1 ♎ 9 ♏	1 ♑ 11 ♒

– VENUS TABLES –

♀	1953	1954	1955	1956	1957	1958	1959	1960
JAN	1 ♒, 6 ♓	1 ♑, 23 ♒	1 ♏, 7 ♐	1 ♒, 18 ♓	1 ♐, 13 ♑	1 ♒	1 ♑, 8 ♒	1 ♏, 3 ♐, 28 ♑
FEB	1 ♓, 3 ♈	1 ♒, 16 ♓	1 ♐, 7 ♑	1 ♓, 12 ♈	1 ♑, 6 ♒	1 ♒	1 ♓, 25 ♈	1 ♑, 21 ♒
MAR	1 ♈, 15 ♉	1 ♓, 12 ♈	1 ♑, 5 ♒, 31 ♓	1 ♈, 8 ♉	1 ♒, 2 ♓, 26 ♈	1 ♒	1 ♈, 21 ♉	1 ♒, 16 ♓
APR	1 ♈	1 ♈, 5 ♉, 29 ♊	1 ♓, 25 ♈	1 ♉, 5 ♊	1 ♈, 19 ♉	1 ♒, 7 ♓	1 ♉, 15 ♊	1 ♓, 10 ♈
MAY	1 ♈	1 ♊, 24 ♋	1 ♈, 20 ♉	1 ♊, 9 ♋	1 ♉, 14 ♊	1 ♓, 6 ♈	1 ♊, 11 ♋	1 ♈, 4 ♉, 29 ♊
JUN	1 ♈, 6 ♉	1 ♋, 18 ♌	1 ♉, 14 ♊	1 ♋, 24 ♊	1 ♊, 7 ♋	1 ♈, 2 ♉, 27 ♊	1 ♋, 7 ♌	1 ♊, 22 ♋
JUL	1 ♉, 8 ♊	1 ♌, 14 ♍	1 ♊, 9 ♋	1 ♊	1 ♋, 2 ♌, 27 ♍	1 ♊, 22 ♋	1 ♌, 9 ♍	1 ♋, 16 ♌
AUG	1 ♊, 5 ♋, 31 ♌	1 ♍, 10 ♎	1 ♋, 2 ♌, 26 ♍	1 ♊, 5 ♋	1 ♍, 21 ♎	1 ♋, 16 ♌	1 ♍	1 ♌, 9 ♍
SEP	1 ♌, 25 ♍	1 ♎, 7 ♏	1 ♍, 19 ♎	1 ♋, 9 ♌	1 ♎, 15 ♏	1 ♌, 10 ♍	1 ♍, 21 ♎, 26 ♍	1 ♍, 3 ♎, 28 ♏
OCT	1 ♍, 19 ♎	1 ♏, 24 ♐, 28 ♏	1 ♎, 13 ♏	1 ♌, 7 ♍	1 ♏, 11 ♐	1 ♍, 3 ♎, 28 ♏	1 ♍	1 ♏, 22 ♐
NOV	1 ♎, 12 ♏	1 ♏	1 ♏, 6 ♐	1 ♍, 26 ♎	1 ♐, 6 ♑	1 ♏, 21 ♐	1 ♍, 10 ♎	1 ♐, 16 ♑
DEC	1 ♏, 6 ♐, 30 ♑	1 ♏	1 ♐, 25 ♑	1 ♎, 20 ♏	1 ♑, 7 ♒	1 ♐, 15 ♑	1 ♎, 8 ♏	1 ♑, 11 ♒

♀	1961	1962	1963	1964	1965	1966	1967	1968
JAN	1 ♒, 6 ♓	1 ♑, 22 ♒	1 ♏, 7 ♐	1 ♒, 17 ♓	1 ♐, 13 ♑	1 ♒	1 ♑, 7 ♒, 31 ♓	1 ♏, 2 ♐, 27 ♑
FEB	1 ♓, 3 ♈	1 ♒, 15 ♓	1 ♐, 6 ♑	1 ♓, 11 ♈	1 ♑, 6 ♒	1 ♒, 7 ♑, 26 ♒	1 ♓, 24 ♈	1 ♑, 21 ♒
MAR	1 ♈	1 ♓, 11 ♈	1 ♑, 5 ♒, 31 ♓	1 ♈, 8 ♉	1 ♒, 2 ♓, 26 ♈	1 ♒	1 ♈, 21 ♉	1 ♒, 16 ♓
APR	1 ♈	1 ♈, 4 ♉, 29 ♊	1 ♓, 25 ♈	1 ♉, 5 ♊	1 ♈, 19 ♉	1 ♒, 7 ♓	1 ♉, 15 ♊	1 ♓, 9 ♈
MAY	1 ♈	1 ♊, 24 ♋	1 ♈, 19 ♉	1 ♊, 10 ♋	1 ♉, 13 ♊	1 ♓, 6 ♈	1 ♊, 11 ♋	1 ♈, 4 ♉, 28 ♊
JUN	1 ♈, 6 ♉	1 ♋, 18 ♌	1 ♉, 13 ♊	1 ♋, 18 ♊	1 ♊, 7 ♋	1 ♈, 2 ♉, 27 ♊	1 ♋, 7 ♌	1 ♊, 21 ♋
JUL	1 ♉, 8 ♊	1 ♌, 13 ♍	1 ♊, 8 ♋	1 ♊	1 ♌, 26 ♍	1 ♊, 22 ♋	1 ♌, 9 ♍	1 ♋, 16 ♌
AUG	1 ♊, 4 ♋, 30 ♌	1 ♍, 9 ♎	1 ♌, 26 ♍	1 ♊, 6 ♋	1 ♍, 20 ♎	1 ♋, 16 ♌	1 ♍	1 ♌, 9 ♍
SEP	1 ♌, 24 ♍	1 ♎, 8 ♏	1 ♍, 18 ♎	1 ♋, 9 ♌	1 ♎, 14 ♏	1 ♌, 9 ♍	1 ♍, 10 ♎	1 ♍, 3 ♎, 27 ♏
OCT	1 ♍, 18 ♎	1 ♏	1 ♎, 13 ♏	1 ♌, 6 ♍	1 ♏, 10 ♐	1 ♍, 3 ♎, 27 ♏	1 ♎, 2 ♍	1 ♏, 22 ♐
NOV	1 ♎, 12 ♏	1 ♏	1 ♏, 6 ♐	1 ♍, 25 ♎	1 ♐, 6 ♑	1 ♏, 20 ♐	1 ♍, 10 ♎	1 ♐, 15 ♑
DEC	1 ♏, 6 ♐, 29 ♑	1 ♏	1 ♐, 24 ♑	1 ♎, 20 ♏	1 ♑, 8 ♒	1 ♐, 14 ♑	1 ♎, 8 ♏	1 ♑, 10 ♒

♀ 1969 – 1976

♀	1969	1970	1971	1972	1973	1974	1975	1976
JAN	1♒ 5♓	1♑ 22♒	1♏ 8♐	1♒ 17♓	1♐ 12♑	1♒ 30♑	1♑ 7♒ 31♓	1♏ 2♐ 27♑
FEB	1♓ 3♈	1♒ 15♓	1♐ 6♑	1♓ 11♈	1♑ 5♒ 28♓	1♑	1♓ 24♈	1♑ 20♒
MAR	1♈	1♓ 11♈	1♑ 5♒ 30♓	1♈ 8♉	1♓ 25♈	1♒	1♈ 20♉	1♒ 15♓
APR	1♈	1♈ 4♉ 28♊	1♓ 24♈	1♉ 4♊	1♈ 19♉	1♒ 7♓	1♉ 14♊	1♓ 9♈
MAY	1♈	1♊ 23♋	1♈ 19♉	1♊ 11♋	1♉ 13♊	1♓ 5♈ 31♉	1♊ 10♋	1♈ 3♉ 27♊
JUN	1♈ 6♉	1♋ 17♌	1♉ 13♊	1♋ 12♊	1♊ 6♋ 30♌	1♉ 25♊	1♋ 7♌	1♊ 21♋
JUL	1♉ 8♊	1♌ 13♍	1♊ 7♋ 31♌	1♊	1♌ 26♍	1♊ 21♋	1♌ 10♍	1♋ 15♌
AUG	1♊ 4♋ 30♌	1♍ 9♎	1♌ 25♍	1♊ 7♋	1♍ 19♎	1♋ 14♌	1♍	1♌ 9♍
SEP	1♌ 24♍	1♎ 8♏	1♍ 18♎	1♋ 8♌	1♎ 14♏	1♌ 8♍	1♍ 3♌	1♍ 2♎ 26♏
OCT	1♍ 18♎	1♏	1♎ 12♏	1♌ 6♍ 31♎	1♏ 10♐	1♍ 2♎ 26♏	1♌ 5♍	1♏ 21♐
NOV	1♎ 11♏	1♏	1♏ 5♐ 30♑	1♎ 25♏	1♐ 6♑	1♏ 19♐	1♍ 10♎	1♐ 14♑
DEC	1♏ 5♐ 29♑	1♏	1♑ 24♒	1♏ 19♐	1♑ 8♒	1♐ 12♑	1♎ 7♏	1♑ 10♒

♀ 1977 – 1984

♀	1977	1978	1979	1980	1981	1982	1983	1984
JAN	1♒ 5♓	1♑ 21♒	1♏ 8♐	1♒ 16♓	1♐ 12♑	1♒ 24♑	1♑ 6♒ 30♓	1♏ 2♐ 26♑
FEB	1♓ 3♈	1♒ 14♓	1♐ 6♑	1♓ 10♈	1♑ 5♒ 28♓	1♑	1♓ 23♈	1♑ 20♒
MAR	1♈	1♓ 10♈	1♑ 4♒ 29♓	1♈ 7♉	1♓ 24♈	1♑ 3♒	1♈ 20♉	1♒ 15♓
APR	1♈	1♈ 3♉ 28♊	1♓ 23♈	1♉ 3♊	1♈ 18♉	1♒ 7♓	1♉ 14♊	1♓ 9♈
MAY	1♈	1♊ 22♋	1♈ 18♉	1♊ 13♋	1♉ 12♊	1♓ 5♈ 31♉	1♊ 10♋	1♈ 3♉ 27♊
JUN	1♈ 7♉	1♋ 17♌	1♉ 12♊	1♋ 6♊	1♊ 6♋ 30♌	1♉ 26♊	1♋ 7♌	1♊ 21♋
JUL	1♉ 7♊	1♌ 12♍	1♊ 7♋ 31♌	1♊	1♌ 25♍	1♊ 21♋	1♌ 11♍	1♋ 15♌
AUG	1♊ 3♋ 29♌	1♍ 8♎	1♌ 25♍	1♊ 6♋	1♍ 19♎	1♋ 15♌	1♍	1♌ 8♍
SEP	1♌ 23♍	1♎ 8♏	1♍ 18♎	1♋ 8♌	1♎ 13♏	1♌ 8♍	1♌	1♍ 2♎ 26♏
OCT	1♍ 17♎	1♏	1♎ 12♏	1♌ 5♍ 31♎	1♏ 9♐	1♍ 2♎ 26♏	1♌ 6♍	1♏ 21♐
NOV	1♎ 11♏	1♏	1♏ 5♐ 29♑	1♎ 25♏	1♐ 6♑	1♏ 19♐	1♍ 10♎	1♐ 14♑
DEC	1♏ 4♐ 28♑	1♏	1♑ 23♒	1♏ 19♐	1♑ 9♒	1♐ 12♑	1♎ 7♏	1♑ 10♒

– VENUS TABLES –

♀	1985	1986	1987	1988	1989	1990	1991	1992
JAN	1 ♒ 5 ♓	1 ♑ 21 ♒	1 ♏ 8 ♐	1 ♒ 16 ♓	1 ♐ 11 ♑	1 ♒ 17 ♑	1 ♑ 6 ♒ 30 ♓	1 ♐ 26 ♑
FEB	1 ♓ 3 ♈	1 ♒ 14 ♓	1 ♐ 6 ♑	1 ♓ 10 ♈	1 ♑ 4 ♒ 28 ♓	1 ♑	1 ♓ 23 ♈	1 ♑ 19 ♒
MAR	1 ♈	1 ♓ 9 ♈	1 ♑ 4 ♒ 29 ♓	1 ♈ 7 ♉	1 ♓ 24 ♈	1 ♑ 4 ♒	1 ♈ 19 ♉	1 ♒ 14 ♓
APR	1 ♈	1 ♈ 3 ♉ 27 ♊	1 ♓ 23 ♈	1 ♉ 4 ♊	1 ♈ 17 ♉	1 ♒ 7 ♓	1 ♉ 13 ♊	1 ♓ 7 ♈
MAY	1 ♈	1 ♊ 22 ♋	1 ♈ 18 ♉	1 ♊ 18 ♋ 27 ♊	1 ♉ 12 ♊	1 ♓ 4 ♈ 31 ♉	1 ♊ 9 ♋	1 ♈ 2 ♉ 26 ♊
JUN	1 ♈ 7 ♉	1 ♋ 16 ♌	1 ♉ 12 ♊	1 ♊	1 ♊ 5 ♋ 30 ♌	1 ♉ 25 ♊	1 ♋ 7 ♌	1 ♊ 20 ♋
JUL	1 ♉ 7 ♊	1 ♌ 13 ♍	1 ♊ 6 ♋ 31 ♌	1 ♊	1 ♌ 24 ♍	1 ♊ 20 ♋	1 ♌ 11 ♍	1 ♋ 14 ♌
AUG	1 ♊ 3 ♋ 28 ♌	1 ♍ 8 ♎	1 ♌ 24 ♍	1 ♊ 7 ♋	1 ♍ 18 ♎	1 ♋ 13 ♌	1 ♍ 22 ♌	1 ♌ 7 ♍
SEP	1 ♌ 23 ♍	1 ♎ 8 ♏	1 ♍ 17 ♎	1 ♋ 8 ♌	1 ♎ 13 ♏	1 ♌ 9 ♍	1 ♌	1 ♎ 25 ♏
OCT	1 ♍ 17 ♎	1 ♏	1 ♎ 11 ♏	1 ♌ 5 ♍ 30 ♎	1 ♏ 9 ♐	1 ♍ 2 ♎ 26 ♏	1 ♌ 7 ♍	1 ♏ 20 ♐
NOV	1 ♎ 10 ♏	1 ♏	1 ♏ 4 ♐ 28 ♑	1 ♎ 24 ♏	1 ♐ 6 ♑	1 ♏ 19 ♐	1 ♍ 9 ♎	1 ♐ 14 ♑
DEC	1 ♏ 4 ♐ 28 ♑	1 ♏	1 ♑ 23 ♒	1 ♏ 18 ♐	1 ♑ 10 ♒	1 ♐ 13 ♑	1 ♎ 7 ♏	1 ♑ 9 ♒

♀	1993	1994	1995	1996	1997	1998	1999	2000
JAN	1 ♒ 4 ♓	1 ♑ 20 ♒	1 ♏ 8 ♐	1 ♒ 15 ♓	1 ♐ 10 ♑	1 ♒ 10 ♑	1 ♑ 5 ♒ 29 ♓	1 ♐ 25 ♑
FEB	1 ♓ 3 ♈	1 ♒ 13 ♓	1 ♐ 5 ♑	1 ♓ 9 ♈	1 ♑ 4 ♒ 28 ♓	1 ♑	1 ♓ 22 ♈	1 ♑ 19 ♒
MAR	1 ♈	1 ♓ 9 ♈	1 ♑ 3 ♒ 29 ♓	1 ♈ 6 ♉	1 ♓ 24 ♈	1 ♑ 5 ♒	1 ♈ 19 ♉	1 ♒ 14 ♓
APR	1 ♈	1 ♈ 2 ♉ 27 ♊	1 ♓ 23 ♈	1 ♉ 4 ♊	1 ♈ 17 ♉	1 ♒ 7 ♓	1 ♉ 13 ♊	1 ♓ 7 ♈
MAY	1 ♈	1 ♊ 21 ♋	1 ♈ 17 ♉	1 ♊	1 ♉ 11 ♊	1 ♓ 4 ♈ 30 ♉	1 ♊ 9 ♋	1 ♈ 2 ♉ 26 ♊
JUN	1 ♈ 7 ♉	1 ♋ 15 ♌	1 ♉ 11 ♊	1 ♊	1 ♊ 4 ♋ 29 ♌	1 ♉ 24 ♊	1 ♋ 6 ♌	1 ♊ 19 ♋
JUL	1 ♉ 6 ♊	1 ♌ 12 ♍	1 ♊ 6 ♋ 30 ♌	1 ♊	1 ♌ 24 ♍	1 ♊ 20 ♋	1 ♌ 13 ♍	1 ♋ 14 ♌
AUG	1 ♊ 2 ♋ 28 ♌	1 ♍ 8 ♎	1 ♌ 23 ♍	1 ♊ 8 ♋	1 ♍ 18 ♎	1 ♋ 14 ♌	1 ♍ 16 ♌	1 ♌ 7 ♍
SEP	1 ♌ 22 ♍	1 ♎ 8 ♏	1 ♍ 17 ♎	1 ♋ 8 ♌	1 ♎ 12 ♏	1 ♌ 7 ♍	1 ♌	1 ♎ 25 ♏
OCT	1 ♍ 16 ♎	1 ♏	1 ♎ 11 ♏	1 ♌ 5 ♍ 30 ♎	1 ♏ 9 ♐	1 ♎ 25 ♏	1 ♌ 8 ♍	1 ♏ 20 ♐
NOV	1 ♎ 9 ♏	1 ♏	1 ♏ 4 ♐ 28 ♑	1 ♎ 23 ♏	1 ♐ 6 ♑	1 ♏ 18 ♐	1 ♍ 10 ♎	1 ♐ 13 ♑
DEC	1 ♏ 3 ♐ 27 ♑	1 ♏	1 ♑ 22 ♒	1 ♏ 17 ♐	1 ♑ 12 ♒	1 ♐ 12 ♑	1 ♎ 6 ♏	1 ♑ 9 ♒

– MARS TABLES –

♂	1921	1922	1923	1924	1925	1926	1927	1928	1929	1930
JAN	1 ♒ 5 ♓	1 ♏	1 ♓ 21 ♈	1 ♏ 19 ♐	1 ♈	1 ♐	1 ♉	1 ♐ 19 ♑	1 ♊	1 ♑
FEB	1 ♓ 13 ♈	1 ♏ 18 ♐	1 ♈	1 ♐	1 ♈ 5 ♉	1 ♐ 9 ♑	1 ♉ 22 ♊	1 ♑ 28 ♒	1 ♊	1 ♑ 6 ♒
MAR	1 ♈ 25 ♉	1 ♐	1 ♈ 4 ♉	1 ♐ 6 ♑	1 ♉ 24 ♊	1 ♑ 23 ♒	1 ♊	1 ♒	1 ♊ 10 ♋	1 ♒ 17 ♓
APR	1 ♉	1 ♐	1 ♉ 16 ♊	1 ♑ 24 ♒	1 ♊	1 ♒	1 ♊ 17 ♋	1 ♒ 7 ♓	1 ♋	1 ♓ 24 ♈
MAY	1 ♉ 6 ♊	1 ♐	1 ♊ 30 ♋	1 ♒	1 ♊ 9 ♋	1 ♒ 3 ♓	1 ♋	1 ♓ 16 ♈	1 ♋ 13 ♌	1 ♈
JUN	1 ♊ 18 ♋	1 ♐	1 ♋	1 ♒ 24 ♓	1 ♋ 26 ♌	1 ♓ 15 ♈	1 ♋ 6 ♌	1 ♈ 26 ♉	1 ♌	1 ♈ 3 ♉
JUL	1 ♋	1 ♐	1 ♋ 16 ♌	1 ♓	1 ♌	1 ♈	1 ♌ 25 ♍	1 ♉	1 ♌ 4 ♍	1 ♉ 14 ♊
AUG	1 ♋ 3 ♌	1 ♐	1 ♌	1 ♓ 24 ♒	1 ♌ 12 ♍	1 ♉	1 ♍	1 ♉ 9 ♊	1 ♍ 21 ♎	1 ♊ 28 ♋
SEP	1 ♌ 19 ♍	1 ♐ 13 ♑	1 ♍	1 ♒	1 ♍ 28 ♎	1 ♉	1 ♍ 10 ♎	1 ♊	1 ♎	1 ♋
OCT	1 ♍	1 ♑ 30 ♒	1 ♍ 18 ♎	1 ♒ 19 ♓	1 ♎	1 ♉	1 ♎ 26 ♏	1 ♊ 3 ♋	1 ♎ 6 ♏	1 ♋ 20 ♌
NOV	1 ♍ 6 ♎	1 ♒	1 ♎	1 ♓	1 ♎ 13 ♏	1 ♉	1 ♏	1 ♋	1 ♏ 18 ♐	1 ♌
DEC	1 ♎ 26 ♏	1 ♒ 11 ♓	1 ♎ 4 ♏	1 ♓ 19 ♈	1 ♏ 28 ♐	1 ♉	1 ♏ 8 ♐	1 ♋ 20 ♊	1 ♐ 29 ♑	1 ♌

♂	1931	1932	1933	1934	1935	1936	1937	1938	1939	1940
JAN	1 ♌	1 ♑ 18 ♒	1 ♍	1 ♒	1 ♎	1 ♒ 14 ♓	1 ♎ 5 ♏	1 ♓ 30 ♈	1 ♏ 29 ♐	1 ♓ 4 ♈
FEB	1 ♌ 16 ♋	1 ♒ 25 ♓	1 ♍	1 ♒ 4 ♓	1 ♎	1 ♓ 22 ♈	1 ♏	1 ♈	1 ♐	1 ♈ 17 ♉
MAR	1 ♋ 30 ♌	1 ♓	1 ♍	1 ♓ 14 ♈	1 ♎	1 ♈	1 ♏ 13 ♐	1 ♈ 12 ♉	1 ♐ 21 ♑	1 ♉
APR	1 ♌	1 ♓ 3 ♈	1 ♍	1 ♈ 22 ♉	1 ♎	1 ♉	1 ♐	1 ♉ 23 ♊	1 ♑	1 ♊
MAY	1 ♌	1 ♈ 12 ♉	1 ♍	1 ♉	1 ♎	1 ♉ 13 ♊	1 ♐	1 ♊	1 ♑ 25 ♒	1 ♊ 17 ♋
JUN	1 ♌ 10 ♍	1 ♉ 8 ♊	1 ♍	1 ♉ 2 ♊	1 ♎	1 ♊ 26 ♋	1 ♐	1 ♊ 7 ♋	1 ♒	1 ♋
JUL	1 ♍	1 ♊	1 ♍ 6 ♎	1 ♊ 15 ♋	1 ♎ 29 ♏	1 ♋	1 ♐	1 ♋ 22 ♌	1 ♒ 21 ♑	1 ♋ 3 ♌
AUG	1 ♎	1 ♊ 4 ♋	1 ♎ 26 ♏	1 ♋ 30 ♌	1 ♏	1 ♋ 10 ♌	1 ♐	1 ♌	1 ♑	1 ♌ 19 ♍
SEP	1 ♎ 17 ♏	1 ♋ 20 ♌	1 ♏	1 ♌	1 ♏ 16 ♐	1 ♌	1 ♐ 30 ♑	1 ♌ 7 ♍	1 ♑ 24 ♒	1 ♍
OCT	1 ♏ 30 ♐	1 ♌	1 ♏ 9 ♐	1 ♌ 18 ♍	1 ♐ 28 ♑	1 ♍	1 ♑	1 ♍ 25 ♎	1 ♒	1 ♍ 5 ♎
NOV	1 ♐	1 ♌ 13 ♍	1 ♐ 19 ♑	1 ♍	1 ♑	1 ♍ 14 ♎	1 ♑ 11 ♒	1 ♎	1 ♒ 19 ♓	1 ♎ 20 ♏
DEC	1 ♐ 10 ♑	1 ♍	1 ♑ 28 ♒	1 ♍ 11 ♎	1 ♑ 11 ♒	1 ♎	1 ♒ 21 ♓	1 ♎ 11 ♏	1 ♓	1 ♏

– MARS TABLES –

♂	1941	1942	1943	1944	1945	1946	1947	1948	1949	1950
JAN	1 ♏ 4 ♐	1 ♈ 11 ♉	1 ♐ 26 ♑	1 ♊	1 ♐ 5 ♑	1 ♋	1 ♑ 25 ♒	1 ♍	1 ♑ 4 ♒	1 ♎
FEB	1 ♐ 17 ♑	1 ♉	1 ♑	1 ♊	1 ♑ 14 ♒	1 ♋	1 ♒	1 ♍ 12 ♌	1 ♒ 11 ♓	1 ♎
MAR	1 ♑	1 ♉ 7 ♊	1 ♑ 8 ♒	1 ♊ 28 ♋	1 ♒ 25 ♓	1 ♋	1 ♒ 4 ♓	1 ♌	1 ♓ 21 ♈	1 ♎ 28 ♍
APR	1 ♑ 2 ♒	1 ♊ 26 ♋	1 ♒ 17 ♓	1 ♋	1 ♓	1 ♋ 22 ♌	1 ♓ 11 ♈	1 ♌	1 ♈ 30 ♉	1 ♍
MAY	1 ♒ 16 ♓	1 ♋	1 ♓ 27 ♈	1 ♋ 22 ♌	1 ♓ 3 ♈	1 ♌	1 ♈ 21 ♉	1 ♌ 18 ♍	1 ♉	1 ♍
JUN	1 ♓	1 ♋ 14 ♌	1 ♈	1 ♌	1 ♈ 11 ♉	1 ♌ 20 ♍	1 ♉	1 ♍	1 ♉ 10 ♊	1 ♍ 11 ♎
JUL	1 ♓ 2 ♈	1 ♌	1 ♈ 7 ♉	1 ♌ 12 ♍	1 ♉ 23 ♊	1 ♍	1 ♊	1 ♍ 17 ♎	1 ♊ 23 ♋	1 ♎
AUG	1 ♈	1 ♍	1 ♉ 23 ♊	1 ♍ 29 ♎	1 ♊	1 ♍ 9 ♎	1 ♊ 13 ♋	1 ♎	1 ♋	1 ♎ 10 ♏
SEP	1 ♈	1 ♍ 17 ♎	1 ♊	1 ♎	1 ♊ 7 ♋	1 ♎ 24 ♏	1 ♋	1 ♎ 3 ♏	1 ♋ 7 ♌	1 ♏ 25 ♐
OCT	1 ♈	1 ♎	1 ♊	1 ♎ 13 ♏	1 ♋	1 ♏	1 ♌	1 ♏ 17 ♐	1 ♌ 27 ♍	1 ♐
NOV	1 ♈	1 ♎ 2 ♏	1 ♊	1 ♏ 25 ♐	1 ♋ 11 ♌	1 ♏ 6 ♐	1 ♌ 20 ♍	1 ♐ 26 ♑	1 ♍	1 ♐ 6 ♑
DEC	1 ♈	1 ♏ 15 ♐	1 ♊	1 ♐	1 ♌ 26 ♋	1 ♐ 17 ♑	1 ♍	1 ♑	1 ♍ 26 ♎	1 ♑ 15 ♒

♂	1951	1952	1953	1954	1955	1956	1957	1958	1959	1960
JAN	1 ♒ 22 ♓	1 ♎ 20 ♏	1 ♓	1 ♏	1 ♒ 15 ♓	1 ♎ 14 ♏	1 ♈ 28 ♉	1 ♐	1 ♉	1 ♐ 14 ♑
FEB	1 ♓	1 ♏	1 ♓ 8 ♈	1 ♏ 9 ♐	1 ♓ 26 ♈	1 ♏ 28 ♐	1 ♉	1 ♐ 3 ♑	1 ♉ 10 ♊	1 ♑ 23 ♒
MAR	1 ♓ 2 ♈	1 ♏	1 ♈ 20 ♉	1 ♐	1 ♈	1 ♐	1 ♉ 17 ♊	1 ♑ 17 ♒	1 ♊	1 ♒
APR	1 ♈ 10 ♉	1 ♏	1 ♉	1 ♐	1 ♈ 11 ♉	1 ♐ 14 ♑	1 ♊	1 ♒ 27 ♓	1 ♊ 10 ♋	1 ♒ 2 ♓
MAY	1 ♉ 21 ♊	1 ♏	1 ♊	1 ♐	1 ♉ 26 ♊	1 ♑	1 ♊ 4 ♋	1 ♓	1 ♋	1 ♓ 11 ♈
JUN	1 ♊	1 ♏	1 ♊ 14 ♋	1 ♐	1 ♊	1 ♑ 3 ♒	1 ♋ 21 ♌	1 ♓ 7 ♈	1 ♋ 2 ♌	1 ♈ 20 ♉
JUL	1 ♊ 3 ♋	1 ♏ 27 ♐	1 ♋ 29 ♌	1 ♐	1 ♊ 11 ♋	1 ♒	1 ♌	1 ♈ 21 ♉	1 ♌ 20 ♍	1 ♉
AUG	1 ♋ 18 ♌	1 ♐	1 ♌	1 ♐	1 ♋ 27 ♌	1 ♒	1 ♌ 8 ♍	1 ♉	1 ♍	1 ♉ 2 ♊
SEP	1 ♌	1 ♐	1 ♌ 14 ♍	1 ♐	1 ♌	1 ♒	1 ♍ 24 ♎	1 ♉ 21 ♊	1 ♍ 5 ♎	1 ♊ 21 ♋
OCT	1 ♌ 5 ♍	1 ♐ 12 ♑	1 ♍	1 ♐ 21 ♑	1 ♌ 13 ♍	1 ♒ 26 ♓	1 ♎	1 ♊ 29 ♉	1 ♎ 21 ♏	1 ♋
NOV	1 ♍ 24 ♎	1 ♑ 21 ♒	1 ♎	1 ♑	1 ♍ 29 ♎	1 ♓	1 ♎ 8 ♏	1 ♉	1 ♏	1 ♋
DEC	1 ♎	1 ♒ 30 ♓	1 ♎ 20 ♏	1 ♑ 4 ♒	1 ♎	1 ♓ 6 ♈	1 ♏ 23 ♐	1 ♉	1 ♏ 3 ♐	1 ♋

– MARS TABLES –

♂	1961	1962	1963	1964	1965	1966	1967	1968	1969	1970
JAN	1 ♋	1 ♑	1 ♌	1 ♑ 13 ♒	1 ♍	1 ♒ 30 ♓	1 ♎	1 ♒ 9 ♓	1 ♏	1 ♓ 24 ♈
FEB	1 ♋ 5 ♊ 7 ♋	1 ♑ 2 ♒	1 ♌	1 ♒ 20 ♓	1 ♍	1 ♓	1 ♎ 12 ♏	1 ♓ 17 ♈	1 ♏ 25 ♐	1 ♈
MAR	1 ♋	1 ♒ 12 ♓	1 ♌	1 ♓ 29 ♈	1 ♍	1 ♓ 9 ♈	1 ♏ 31 ♎	1 ♈ 28 ♉	1 ♐	1 ♈ 7 ♉
APR	1 ♋	1 ♓ 19 ♈	1 ♌	1 ♈	1 ♍	1 ♈ 17 ♉	1 ♎	1 ♉	1 ♐	1 ♉ 18 ♊
MAY	1 ♋ 6 ♌	1 ♈ 28 ♉	1 ♌	1 ♈ 7 ♉	1 ♍	1 ♉ 28 ♊	1 ♎	1 ♉ 8 ♊	1 ♐	1 ♊
JUN	1 ♌ 28 ♍	1 ♉	1 ♌ 3 ♍	1 ♉ 17 ♊	1 ♍ 29 ♎	1 ♊	1 ♎	1 ♊ 21 ♋	1 ♐	1 ♊ 2 ♋
JUL	1 ♍	1 ♉ 9 ♊	1 ♍ 27 ♎	1 ♊ 30 ♋	1 ♎	1 ♊ 11 ♋	1 ♎ 19 ♏	1 ♋	1 ♐	1 ♋ 18 ♌
AUG	1 ♍ 17 ♎	1 ♊ 22 ♋	1 ♎	1 ♋	1 ♎ 20 ♏	1 ♋ 25 ♌	1 ♏	1 ♋ 5 ♌	1 ♐	1 ♌
SEP	1 ♎	1 ♋	1 ♎ 12 ♏	1 ♋	1 ♏	1 ♌	1 ♏ 21 ♐	1 ♌ 21 ♍	1 ♐ 21 ♑	1 ♌ 3 ♍
OCT	1 ♎ 2 ♏	1 ♋ 11 ♌	1 ♏ 25 ♐	1 ♌	1 ♏ 4 ♐	1 ♌ 12 ♍	1 ♐ 23 ♑	1 ♍	1 ♑	1 ♍ 20 ♎
NOV	1 ♏ 13 ♐	1 ♌	1 ♐	1 ♌ 6 ♍	1 ♐ 14 ♑	1 ♍	1 ♑	1 ♍ 9 ♎	1 ♑ 4 ♒	1 ♎
DEC	1 ♐ 24 ♑	1 ♌	1 ♐ 5 ♑	1 ♍	1 ♑ 23 ♒	1 ♍ 4 ♎	1 ♑ 2 ♒	1 ♎ 30 ♏	1 ♒ 15 ♓	1 ♎ 6 ♏

♂	1971	1972	1973	1974	1975	1976	1977	1978	1979	1980
JAN	1 ♏ 23 ♐	1 ♈	1 ♐	1 ♉	1 ♐ 21 ♑	1 ♊	1 ♑	1 ♌ 26 ♋	1 ♑ 21 ♒	1 ♍
FEB	1 ♐	1 ♈ 10 ♉	1 ♐ 12 ♑	1 ♉ 27 ♊	1 ♑	1 ♊	1 ♑ 9 ♒	1 ♋	1 ♒ 28 ♓	1 ♍
MAR	1 ♐ 12 ♑	1 ♉ 27 ♊	1 ♑ 27 ♒	1 ♊	1 ♑ 3 ♒	1 ♊ 18 ♋	1 ♒ 20 ♓	1 ♋	1 ♓	1 ♍ 12 ♌
APR	1 ♑	1 ♊	1 ♒	1 ♊ 20 ♋	1 ♒ 11 ♓	1 ♋	1 ♓ 28 ♈	1 ♋ 11 ♌	1 ♓ 7 ♈	1 ♌
MAY	1 ♑ 3 ♒	1 ♊ 12 ♋	1 ♒ 8 ♓	1 ♋	1 ♓ 21 ♈	1 ♋ 16 ♌	1 ♈	1 ♌	1 ♈ 16 ♉	1 ♌ 4 ♍
JUN	1 ♒	1 ♋ 28 ♌	1 ♓ 21 ♈	1 ♋ 9 ♌	1 ♈	1 ♌	1 ♈ 6 ♉	1 ♌ 14 ♍	1 ♉ 26 ♊	1 ♍
JUL	1 ♒	1 ♌	1 ♈	1 ♌ 27 ♍	1 ♉	1 ♌ 7 ♍	1 ♉ 18 ♊	1 ♍	1 ♊	1 ♍ 11 ♎
AUG	1 ♒	1 ♌ 15 ♍	1 ♈ 12 ♉	1 ♍	1 ♉ 14 ♊	1 ♍ 24 ♎	1 ♊	1 ♍ 4 ♎	1 ♊ 8 ♋	1 ♎ 29 ♏
SEP	1 ♒	1 ♍	1 ♉	1 ♍ 12 ♎	1 ♊	1 ♎	1 ♋	1 ♎ 20 ♏	1 ♋ 25 ♌	1 ♏
OCT	1 ♒	1 ♎	1 ♉ 30 ♊	1 ♎ 28 ♏	1 ♊ 17 ♋	1 ♎ 9 ♏	1 ♋ 27 ♌	1 ♏	1 ♌	1 ♏ 12 ♐
NOV	1 ♒ 6 ♓	1 ♎ 15 ♏	1 ♊	1 ♏	1 ♋ 26 ♊	1 ♏ 21 ♐	1 ♌	1 ♏ 2 ♐	1 ♌ 20 ♍	1 ♐ 22 ♑
DEC	1 ♓ 26 ♈	1 ♏ 30 ♐	1 ♊ 24 ♉	1 ♏ 11 ♐	1 ♊	1 ♐	1 ♌	1 ♐ 13 ♑	1 ♍	1 ♑ 31 ♒

♂	1981	1982	1983	1984	1985	1986	1987	1988	1989	1990
JAN	1 ♒	1 ♎	1 ♒ 17 ♓	1 ♎ 11 ♏	1 ♓	1 ♏	1 ♓ 8 ♈	1 ♏ 9 ♐	1 ♈ 19 ♉	1 ♐ 30 ♑
FEB	1 ♒ 7 ♓	1 ♎	1 ♓ 25 ♈	1 ♏	1 ♓ 3 ♈	1 ♏ 2 ♐	1 ♈ 21 ♉	1 ♐ 22 ♑	1 ♉	1 ♑
MAR	1 ♓ 17 ♈	1 ♎	1 ♈	1 ♏	1 ♈ 15 ♉	1 ♐ 28 ♑	1 ♉	1 ♑	1 ♉ 11 ♊	1 ♑ 12 ♒
APR	1 ♈ 25 ♉	1 ♎	1 ♈ 5 ♉	1 ♏	1 ♉ 26 ♊	1 ♑	1 ♉ 6 ♊	1 ♑ 7 ♒	1 ♊ 29 ♋	1 ♒ 21 ♓
MAY	1 ♉	1 ♎	1 ♉ 17 ♊	1 ♏	1 ♊	1 ♑	1 ♊ 21 ♋	1 ♒ 22 ♓	1 ♋	1 ♓ 31 ♈
JUN	1 ♉ 5 ♊	1 ♎	1 ♊ 29 ♋	1 ♏	1 ♊ 9 ♋	1 ♑	1 ♋	1 ♓	1 ♋ 17 ♌	1 ♈
JUL	1 ♊ 18 ♋	1 ♎	1 ♋	1 ♏	1 ♋ 25 ♌	1 ♑	1 ♋ 7 ♌	1 ♓ 14 ♈	1 ♌	1 ♈ 13 ♉
AUG	1 ♋	1 ♎ 3 ♏	1 ♋ 14 ♌	1 ♏ 18 ♐	1 ♌	1 ♑	1 ♌ 23 ♍	1 ♈	1 ♌ 3 ♍	1 ♉ 31 ♊
SEP	1 ♋ 2 ♌	1 ♏ 20 ♐	1 ♌ 30 ♍	1 ♐	1 ♌ 10 ♍	1 ♑	1 ♍	1 ♈	1 ♍ 20 ♎	1 ♊
OCT	1 ♌ 21 ♍	1 ♐	1 ♍	1 ♐ 5 ♑	1 ♍ 28 ♎	1 ♑ 9 ♒	1 ♍ 9 ♎	1 ♈ 24 ♓	1 ♎	1 ♊
NOV	1 ♍	1 ♑	1 ♍ 18 ♎	1 ♑ 16 ♒	1 ♎	1 ♒ 26 ♓	1 ♎ 24 ♏	1 ♓ 2 ♈	1 ♎ 4 ♏	1 ♊
DEC	1 ♍ 16 ♎	1 ♑ 10 ♒	1 ♎	1 ♒ 25 ♓	1 ♎ 15 ♏	1 ♓	1 ♏	1 ♈	1 ♏ 18 ♐	1 ♊ 14 ♉

♂	1991	1992	1993	1994	1995	1996	1997	1998	1999	2000
JAN	1 ♉ 21 ♊	1 ♐ 9 ♑	1 ♋	1 ♑ 28 ♒	1 ♍ 23 ♌	1 ♑ 9 ♒	1 ♍ 3 ♎	1 ♒ 25 ♓	1 ♎ 26 ♏	1 ♒ 4 ♓
FEB	1 ♊	1 ♑ 18 ♒	1 ♋	1 ♒	1 ♌	1 ♒ 15 ♓	1 ♎	1 ♓	1 ♏	1 ♓ 12 ♈
MAR	1 ♊	1 ♒ 28 ♓	1 ♋	1 ♒ 7 ♓	1 ♌	1 ♓ 25 ♈	1 ♎ 9 ♍	1 ♓ 5 ♈	1 ♏	1 ♈ 23 ♉
APR	1 ♊ 3 ♋	1 ♓	1 ♋ 28 ♌	1 ♓ 15 ♈	1 ♌	1 ♈	1 ♍	1 ♈ 13 ♉	1 ♏	1 ♉
MAY	1 ♋ 27 ♌	1 ♓ 6 ♈	1 ♌	1 ♈ 24 ♉	1 ♌ 25 ♍	1 ♈ 3 ♉	1 ♍	1 ♉ 24 ♊	1 ♏ 6 ♎	1 ♉ 4 ♊
JUN	1 ♌	1 ♈ 15 ♉	1 ♌ 23 ♍	1 ♉	1 ♍	1 ♉ 12 ♊	1 ♍ 19 ♎	1 ♊	1 ♎	1 ♊ 16 ♋
JUL	1 ♌ 16 ♍	1 ♉ 27 ♊	1 ♍	1 ♉ 4 ♊	1 ♍ 21 ♎	1 ♊ 26 ♋	1 ♎	1 ♊ 6 ♋	1 ♎ 5 ♏	1 ♋
AUG	1 ♍	1 ♊	1 ♍ 12 ♎	1 ♊ 17 ♋	1 ♎	1 ♋	1 ♎ 14 ♏	1 ♋ 21 ♌	1 ♏	1 ♌
SEP	1 ♎	1 ♊ 12 ♋	1 ♎ 27 ♏	1 ♋	1 ♎ 7 ♏	1 ♋ 10 ♌	1 ♏ 29 ♐	1 ♌	1 ♏ 3 ♐	1 ♌ 17 ♍
OCT	1 ♎ 17 ♏	1 ♋	1 ♏	1 ♋ 5 ♌	1 ♏ 21 ♐	1 ♌ 30 ♍	1 ♐	1 ♌ 7 ♍	1 ♐ 17 ♑	1 ♍
NOV	1 ♏ 29 ♐	1 ♋	1 ♏ 9 ♐	1 ♌	1 ♐ 30 ♑	1 ♍	1 ♐ 9 ♑	1 ♍ 27 ♎	1 ♑ 27 ♒	1 ♍ 4 ♎
DEC	1 ♐	1 ♋	1 ♐ 20 ♑	1 ♌ 12 ♍	1 ♑	1 ♍	1 ♑ 18 ♒	1 ♎	1 ♒	1 ♎ 23 ♏